How

7 Easy Steps to Master Mind Mapping Techniques, Note-taking, Creative Thinking & Brainstorming Skills

Troye Bates

More by Troye Bates

Discover all books from the Brain Training Series by Troye Bates at:

bit.ly/troye-bates

Book 1: *How to Improve Memory*

Book 2: *How to Read Faster*

Book 3: *How to Focus Your Mind*

Book 4: *How to Learn Faster*

Book 5: *How to Study Effectively*

Book 6: *How to Mind Map*

Book 7: *How to Think Differently*

Book 8: *How to Rewire Your Brain*

Themed book bundles available at discounted prices:

bit.ly/troye-bates

Copyright

Table of Contents

Introduction

The Mind Mapping concept has been around for quite some time. Mind Mapping has grown in its reputation, especially within the academic circles. This concept was formerly used as a means of bringing out a sense of large pieces of information, and it has since been accepted and applied in various fields and industries.

Mind Mapping is a great weapon that you need in your arsenal if you are looking for ways to achieve your goals or take your career to the next level. If you have different ways to represent information that people wouldn't even think about, you already have a clear advantage! In no time, you will see your productivity go off the charts when you learn and apply the things described in this guide.

The term "Mind Map" was first popularized by Tony Buzan who formalized Mind Maps as a way to look at information differently. The different views allow users to have different perspectives, which gives them more clarity, better insight, understanding, and peace of mind. For a long time, people have used mapping structures to represent information, then Tony Buzan formalized it by giving it a name!

Mind Mapping is a blend of art and science, words and images, emotion and logic. All these are well blended to give us the result – Mind Maps. Luckily, Mind Mapping is something our brain likes.

The following chapters will discuss:

- What Mind Mapping is, its uses, and getting started with it.
- The different applications of a Mind Map.
- The Mind Mapping techniques.
- How to create a Mind Map?
- The principles and laws guiding Mind Maps.
- 7 step system to help you mastering Mind Mapping techniques.

Whether it's in your career, at school, or in your personal life, Mind Mapping will significantly increase your productivity and help you achieve your set goals. If you are new to Mind Mapping, this guide will give you all the information you need to master Mind Mapping techniques. Every effort was made to ensure it is full of as much useful information as possible; please enjoy it!

Chapter 1: Introduction to Mind Mapping

Remember what they say about the power of a great idea? Well, the power of every great idea lies in its simplicity. As opposed to the traditional ways of linear text and note-taking, a Mind Map structures information in a way that closely resembles how our brain works. Mind Mapping is an activity that is artistic and analytical; this makes our brain engaged in a better way and helps in all cognitive functions. And the best part of it all is that Mind Mapping is fun!

So, what really is a Mind Map, and what does it look like?

What Is Mind Mapping?

The ultimate tool of an organized thought process is a Mind Map. It's the easiest way of putting information into your brain and taking information out of your brain — it's a creative and effective way to take note that literally 'maps' your thoughts." Mind Mapping has come a long way since its introduction. It has even become a mainstream tool that is being used by academic students, business professionals, and many other individuals. Commonly it is used to manage, organize, and reimage information in a unique and highly structured way.

Clear
Associations
Radiant
Hierarchical
Structure
Fun
EMPHASIS
Style
Personal
Beauty

Paper
Blank
Landscape
Start

Mind Maps

Use
Images
Colour
Words

Connect
Thicker
Length
Organic
Lines

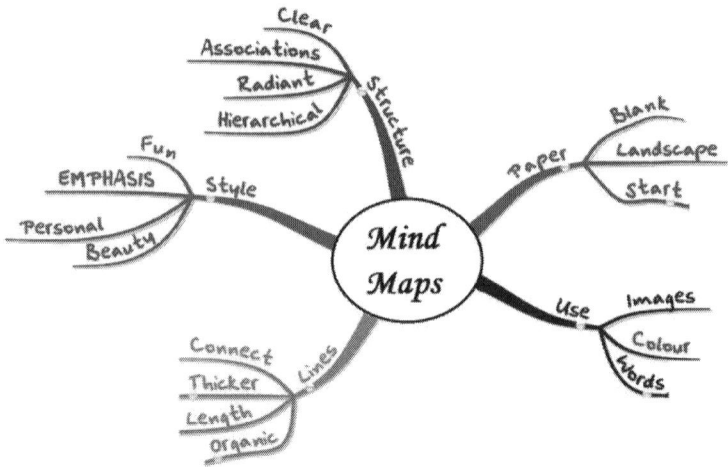

There are so many shades of definition to the term, 'Mind Mapping'. However, the best and most accurate description was what its pioneer, Tony Buzan, defined. Mind Mapping can be defined as a visual information management tool that aids business, working professionals, and students to memorize, arrange, structure, brainstorm, and learn information in a skilled and specialized way.

The last two decades have brought the human race to an incredible realm of knowledge utilizing the human mind and our limitless capacity to think, comprehend, and store vast information. Meanwhile, recent studies have shown that the human capacity to think effectively and quickly is closely related to our imagination and our ability to create associations between various chunks of information.

Nevertheless, Mind Mapping these days is not just about making a map. Instead, it has evolved into a visual information management tool that transforms our way of thinking, working, and developing our capacity for visible reflection. In a Mind Map, data is structured in a way that fits well with how the brain functions. This is opposed to traditional note-taking or static script because it involves both intellectual and creativity. Mind Mapping stimulates the mind in a much more productive manner and assists with all its cognitive functions.

Mind Mapping is a process by which information is stored, arranged, prioritized, updated, checked, and preserved. This provides a description or analysis of a body of knowledge that incorporates words and pictures. Mind Mapping effortlessly combines reasoning with creative thinking to help us feel the topic we are studying more skillfully and efficiently.

Mind Mapping Facts

Mind Mapping has been in use since ancient times, and as we become more aware and mentally informed, more people are beginning to come in contact and adopting the use of Mind Mapping. This is the ultimate mind and memory power tool to stimulate your brain for more potentials to make great progress in your endeavors. The need for more brainpower is expanding, and people are turning to Mind Mapping for the effective and efficient use of their brain potentials to improve their productivity.

Mind Map has helped in the creation, development, and advancement of cutting edge technologies, equipment, and devices.

Fact #1

One of the new Boeing Aircraft was created using a Mind Map, and a lot of people don't know this fact of people. According to a CNN report, Boeing was able to save about $11 million using Mind Maps while working on the new designs for their Aircraft. Interestingly, the Boeing Aircraft Engineering Manual was compressed into a 25 feet long Mind Map.

This enabled a team of one hundred aeronautical engineers to learn what would have taken a few years in just a few weeks, saving them a whole lot of money.

Fact #2

The former United States Vice President, Al Gore, uses Mind Mapping application software to organize his thoughts in proper order. Al Gore has been awarded Nobel Peace Prize, and he holds many high profile positions in reputable companies like Apple Inc., Google, Alliance for Climate Protection, and many more. He was featured on the cover of the May/June 2007 issue of Time Magazine, with a featured article that showed the photograph of the former US Vice President, Al Gore, while his project Mind Map was in front of him.

Using Mind Maps as a tool, he could effectively manage information in order to make and execute import decisions. There are so many tasks that require his attention to be accomplished at certain times of the day, so he employs Mind Maps to help him remember all these important tasks every day.

Fact #3

Former Microsoft President Bill Gates, who used to be known as the world's richest man and one of the world's most brilliant minds, was because of his brainpower. In his younger days, he dropped out of Harvard University in order to build his computer and achieve his dream with his partner Paul Allen.

Bill Gates stated that Mind Mapping would usher the world into the next stage of new information management. In recent times, Mind Maps can be said to be one of the most powerful tools to manage information because it organizes information easily and logically to remember a lot of things.

Elements of a Mind Map

Mind Map elements are quite simple. There usually is a central core node that represents a topic, an image, or a central idea. Let's refer to this as the 'Central Topic.' When you have a central topic, various branches can stem from other nodes and topics. These branches are typically represented with relationship lines or arrows that lead to other topics.

To explain or make things simpler to understand, we will be referring to the first nodes from the central topic as the 'main topics,' and every other node or group of nodes will be further referred to as 'subtopics.' Each of the branches from the central topic can become multiple main topics and subtopics. Remember that you can only have a single central topic, and never more than that one, having more than one central topic would mean the creation of a separate Mind Map.

There are permanent links or relationships between the central topic and the main topics, the same way that there are permanent links or relationships between the main topics and the corresponding subtopics. Therefore, all of the connected main topics should actually define the central topic. To simply put, if all the main topics are summed together, each of the main topics should flow with the central topic and should be able to describe it in full.

You should be able to put together and place your main topics in such a way that they would clearly define what the central topic is – you would also be able to tell what the central topic is all about just by reading the main topics. The same thing should apply to your subtopics and the main topics.

You can cluster together things that are closely related to the main topic. That way, you can have several subtopics that constitute the main topic. Let's use a real-life example to demonstrate this point.

Walt Disney used a range of Mind Maps to communicate new ideas and concepts with others. Let's say he was trying to share his vision for Disney and communicate his ideas to others. **DISNEY** would become the central topic, then the main topic leading out from there would be **Disneyland, Disney TV,** and **Merchandising.** Other clusters of subtopics branching from **Disneyland's** main topic would then be subtopics like *Frontier Land, Adventure Land,* and *Tomorrow Land.*

With such elements, it is evident that this would be great for planning purposes. This method was how Walt Disney was able to entirely oversee all his projects, ranging from books, comics, music, movies, licensing, theme parks, and the rest of his merchandise. Through the use of Mind Maps, Walt was able to oversee an entire complex system and in a much simpler manner. This allowed his business to thrive and become one of the most successful in the world.

Hand-Drawn vs. Computerized Mind Maps

When creating a Mind Map, you don't always need a sophisticated computer program to achieve the desired results. With a standard sheet of paper, you can quickly draw out a Mind Map. This method is quicker, cheaper, and easier when making a Mind Map. Then again, there has been an explosive increase in the number of computerized methods and Mind Mapping tools available, and we have also found them very convenient and useful.

Using the computerized methods of creating Mind Maps presents more flexibility because you can organize and reorganize different main topics and subtopics as much as you want just by dragging and dropping them. Your Mind Maps main topics, subtopics, and nodes are also very easy to color code. This advantage allows you to easily and flexibly create several relationships between the main topics and the subtopics – this will help you to easily simplify Mind Maps with very complex systems in a clear and easy to recognize way.

Although drawing is not a prerequisite for either the hand-drawn or computerized method of creating Mind Maps, but Mind Mapping programs make it easier with the flexibility of using a picture to represent or symbolize different points and topics in the Mind Map. As a matter of fact, there are lots and lots of illustrations, images, and graphic materials that can be utilized. With the numerous types of flowcharts images available, you can easily express the relationship between the topics clearly.

You can also print out a chart to carry around if you need to. Therefore, you have the opportunity to own both a digital and hard copy that you can use or store as the situation demands. Meaning when you are on the run or going somewhere, you won't be able to access your computer; you can have your Mind Map printed out and carry with you for use. Alternatively, you can as well carry a digital copy with you and access it on another computer, mail yourself a copy where you can access anywhere you are.

If you start your Mind Maps using the hand-draw method, you will do more of sketching on paper as you go through your day. However, if you are using Mind Mapping software, you will be inclined to use your computer more often since you can make clearer and more creative forms of Mind Maps using software.

Different Ways You Can Put Mind Maps Together

Mind Maps are very flexible, and it is one of the reasons they are really great to use. You can use them in a variety of ways, and there are a lot of ways you can put Mind Maps together. Let's take a look at three different approaches that you can use in putting Mind Maps together.

Open & Get Cracking

To get started with this approach, all you need to do is put your central topic on a paper, then draw out a few lines that will be leading to your main topics, then you can let your ideas start flowing, using the tools at your disposal to build it up. This method is a very basic one, where you start with an idea and then begin building from the ground to up. This method is very suitable when you use Mind Maps to come up with ideas.

Take Notes & Then Mind Map

This method begins by taking notes and gathering the necessary information you will need, after that, you can then formulate a Mind Map out of the gathered information from the notes you have taken, and as you proceed you will be categorizing the information. Apparently, this approach is a little more advanced compared to the previous approach because you will be starting will a pool of information instead of just diving right in. This method works best when you plan things out, then communicate your ideas.

Different Levels of Involvement

This third approach entails the use and reuse of information. This approach is suitable when you have an existing Mind Map, or there are requirements for different levels for different needs. This approach will let you use different templates that already exist and are available, or you could just add to an old Mind Map. This is basically taking an already existing information, edit it, adjust it in different ways, and then use it.

This method lets you learn content better since you are working with an existing template; it lets you reclassify the information based on the new ideas and concepts you have formed. You could even have several Mind Maps open and make use of two or more of them at the same time so that you can add or combine the best information from

18

the Mind Maps. This approach is best used with a computerized program for Mind Mapping if you can, but you don't always have to.

Why You Should Use Mind Maps

Mind Maps are a great tool to create ideas, plan your life, schedule, etc. These ten uses mentioned before for Mind Maps are just the beginning. Live your best life by using Mind Maps to activate your entire mind power. Let's take a look at some of the reasons why you should use Mind Maps.

Using Mind Maps Will Provide Engagement for You

Mind Mapping system encourages more significant involvement of participants similar to a whiteboard. Everything is much simpler on a Mind Map – not only the comments themselves but also the similarities between those comments and main chart topics. As a result, members can see the project fully, develop their feedback, and contribute additional ideas that are also applied to the emerging program.

Using Mind Maps Allows for More Flexibility

The simplicity with which ideas can be clustered and transferred around a monitor in real-time during the planning session is one of the main benefits of a Mind Map over a whiteboard. It is not only feasible to treat single topics and feedback this way – it is also possible to quickly transfer, restructure, and attach whole sections of multiple issues to the graph.

Using Mind Maps Gives You Speed and Accuracy

At brainstorming sessions, using Mind Mapping makes it easier to stay on track than those utilizing conventional whiteboards. Most rely on the facilitator's expertise, of course, but Mind Mapping provides some practical benefits. Also, the facilitator will move much faster through the day of preparation without having to stop periodically to clear the screen for the next subject to be published.

Additionally, the facilitator may quickly and accurately apply participant responses to the map; eventually, when thoughts are incorporated, a Mind Map can be extended on-screen. Compare it with using a whiteboard, where the meeting must be interrupted whenever the board is complete so that it can be captured for one or more images and then discarded so that the planning process can begin.

Using Mind Maps Helps Increase Your Focus

As a facilitator, you can use a Mind Map to highlight specific topics for discussion, temporarily "disappearing" the rest of the plan. This makes it much easier for everyone to stay on track. Alternatively, through multiple topics, the facilitator may present a whole section, letting team members understand how they are connected. This is also a useful tool to demonstrate subjects that require solutions, which means that more thought and feedback from the audience may be required.

Using Mind Maps Helps for Easy Adaptability

Whiteboards are stationary for the most part. Even if it is on wheels, it is guaranteed that the whiteboard of your organization spends most of its time in your meeting room; everything that anyone does with it is typically transcribed to useful results somewhere. While some tools are available to assist in this phase, the principle stays mostly the same.

Certain features of Mind Mapping technology, besides acting as a thought and planning tool, contribute to its ultimate Adaptability. In many instances, the Mind Map can be turned into an interactive resource. Specific features differ from software to system, but most of the more advanced Mind Mapping applications require you to insert task-related data for each of the activities listed in a planning session, such as start and end times, finances, goals, and progress to date.

Using Mind Maps Will Make You Very Efficient

Some of the features listed before also lead to a Mind Map's other benefit over a whiteboard–efficiency. For instance, at the end of the session, the facilitator does not need to spend much time transcribing a scrawl of handwritten notes–the content is already there, typed up, and preparation of final editing. This means that the results can be produced much faster, even after the planning session is over immediately.

Using Mind Map Allows for Smooth Transparency

With a Mind Map, people can easily see if the facilitator or scribe accurately records their ideas and how their ideas relate to their peers' previous comments. Also, as the planning day progresses, the facilitator can print or even email summary snapshots of the evolving map to participants in real-time. This method will help us appreciate how the meeting session formed the conversations. After the course is over, respondents will equate the images with the final write-up to see how the outcomes integrated their replies.

Getting Started on Mind Mapping

Imagination and association are the two fundamental things that the brain requires for learning to take place in psychology. According to Tony Buzan, it is nothing new. The Greeks devised an active memory system based on association and imagination as well, that enabled them to remember hundreds, and sometimes, thousands of facts.

While researching the Greeks, Leonardo Da Vinci and other creative people was just how Tony Buzan came up with the idea of Mind Maps: a visual depiction of information — using creativity and association to catch plans and projects in a manner that can be easily remembered, interpreted and clarified.

All Mind Maps start at the core (of a page or a screen, etc.), and, from there, divisions emanate forth. Mind Maps are bright, sometimes colorful, too, and full of lines, symbols, words, and images that help organize information for our brains. Buzan suggests that "With a Mind Map, you could transform a long list of repetitive details into a fun, unforgettable, highly organized diagram that fits under the natural way you do stuff in your head."

So, what are we going to need to create a Mind Map? We will need a white paper, colored pens, pencils, and of course our creativity. Many people have often done it on the back of a black eyeliner napkin in a hurry, any pen or pencil will do it. However, there are many other online/offline applications or computer solutions you can use.

Mind Maps will help you be more imaginative, conserve time, resolve issues, reflect, coordinate and explain your thoughts, pass good grade tests, learn more, practice faster and more effectively, research a breeze, see the full picture,' schedule, connect," and most importantly, yield results!

Creativity Yields Result

An essential principle of the Mind Mapping system is that creativity yields a result called a 'product' in the process. Subsequently, you will eventually see that the result can be a painting, a theory, or a new electrical device. However, different products may appear, and they are a concrete result. Creativity is, therefore, more than just the development of original ideas. If ideas are not used for something, then they're worthless.

Anyone can be creative about everything. The central message: everyone can be innovative, and every mentally sound adult can be creative. Except for highly talented people with special talents, genetics has no role to play here. The assertion, ' I'm not creative' doesn't sit well here.

Action: Think about a project or idea you've got to deal with. Use a Mind Map to capture it on paper. It would help if you kept Mind Mapping as a handy tool for managing information or turning the complex into a piece of simple-to-see information and understand the mechanism. For many years now, many people have been using Mind Mapping, and the clarity and organization it brings to their jumbled thoughts always helps them to understand the structure of their projects better.

Chapter 2: Applications of Mind Mapping

Almost everyone needs Mind Mapping for everyday purposes, like planning and organizing. If you don't want to do so much and achieve little at the end of the day, Mind Mapping is for you. It maximizes your potential, gives you a clear idea of what you want to accomplish, helps you solve problems with ease, and makes it easier for you to present your ideas to others for teamwork.

The idea of Mind Mapping evolved from Porphyry in the 3rd century and was made famous by a renowned psychologist from Britain, Tony Buzan. However, in practice, Mind Mapping applications evolve from our thoughts. When we visit a new place or experience new things, our mind awakes, and new ideas flow out. We try to relate these thoughts with memory to determine if we can accept or reject such thoughts. From one memory to another memory, the central idea that was triggered would eventually mean a lot of things to you: this is the whole concept of Mind Mapping. A central idea is linked to several ideas like a tree branch.

In corporate organizations, Mind Mapping starts as brainstorming sessions — the session results in a list of disorganized information. However, after going through Mind Mapping techniques, the fractals become a vital resource for many project managers.

Alternative solutions   Impact analysis

Issues

Decision making   Root causes

Alternatives   Problem solving   Quality   Profitability

Project management   **Brainstorming**   Improves   Initiative

Ideas and possibilities   Innovation

Team building   Morale   Efficiency

Share discussions

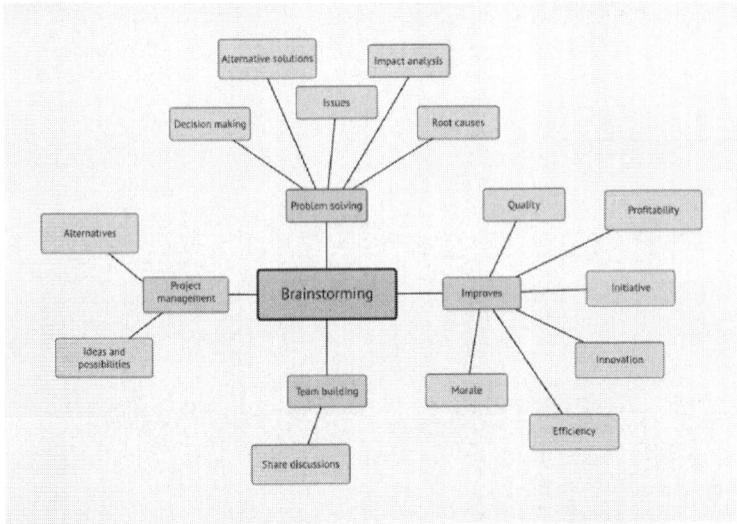

The Mind Map is represented with colorful presentations that can capture the idea. It is more than just written words and diagrams with little or no meanings. The central idea is always big at the center, presented in such a way that shows its importance. Other smaller concepts and the way they are related to the central thought should be around the main concept. Think of it like a tree (central idea) and its branches (other related ideas).

You can apply the Mind Map in the following ways:

Brainstorming

Many writers are told to brainstorm when they are about to write. The reason is apparent; brainstorming is like a trigger that jumpstart ideas out of the brain. If you lack creative and innovative ideas, the act of brainstorming will help you find these unique ideas. When brainstorming, you are allowing free-flowing thoughts to control your pen. The information you get when you brainstorm is not always organized and accurate: this is why you have to do a full analysis of the ideas generated.

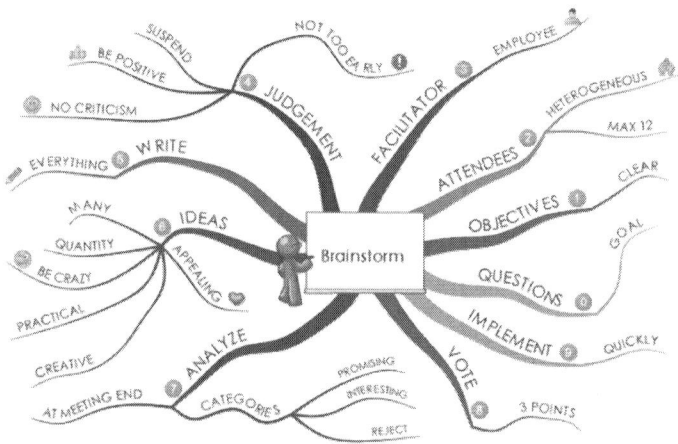

Mind Mapping is an effective way to brainstorm. Mind Mapping and brainstorming have the same function. However, Mind Mapping brainstorming is more efficient than just brainstorming as it also saves you time. Many project managers use Mind Mapping brainstorming to overcome information overload, and it also helps them organize information faster. There are some rules to follow for this:

First and foremost, allow thoughts to go out free from your head, and this is one basic rule of brainstorming. Don't restrain your ideas; don't tell yourself that an idea is ridiculous or fantastic; don't tell yourself anything. Just allow thoughts to flow as you write them down. In this way, strategic thoughts, as well as creative ones, will fill your paper; you will be surprised at how many ideas you can produce.

Organize your ideas after writing them down. Don't forget to stop prejudging any written plan: don't tell yourself anything. Begin by arranging the opinions on any basis you like, but you must be aware of the goal you want to accomplish or the central purpose.

Fix your mind on the primary goal when brainstorming: this is important because it is possible to miss the whole point when you allow your mind to wander freely. To be purposeful in brainstorming, allow your mind to revolve around the main idea freely. Think as you want, but think about the goal.

Decision Making

Most entrepreneurs depend on the outcome of excellent decision-making skills to succeed. Picking up just any innovative ideas available can be disastrous. Therefore, the entrepreneur faces the difficult task of making decisions, and he cannot avoid it. In making decisions effectively, entrepreneurs gather ideas, follow trends, and think creatively as well as strategically.

The major problem in decision-making is uncertain outcomes. You can easily make decisions when you already know the result but, knowing the effect is only in theory. The problem can only be cut short by getting updated knowledge, data, facts, and ideas about the decision: this is where Mind Mapping is vital in making critical decisions.

The ease at which ideas are generated and presented in a Mind Map makes it easy to perform a proper assessment before deciding an action. The visuals, images, and words presented around the central idea help every project manager to quickly understand a concept without which he would make wrong decisions. Time is also the primary factor in decision-making; poor decision-making skills include sluggishness in choosing a line of action. Any good decision-making entrepreneur can be slow in making decisions, most notably when the information he has is difficult to comprehend, and he finds it hard to make inferences.

Organizing Information

There is an explosion of information in the world today. The problem is not just that there is so much to know, but it is now straightforward to access this information. To make matters worse, knowledge seems to be increasing every day with different updates and changes. The explosion of information has made learning very difficult, as it can be tough to find the right information without emptying your purse. Therefore, today, if you want to learn anything, the first you do is to organize the information you want to learn.

Mind Mapping helps us to organize information effectively: this is a crucial tool for learning. Mind Mapping helps you to know what information you need and the ones that are useful for you. Writers and project researchers are always involved in information gathering. Most of the times, these people tend to deviate from the particular information of interest. Due to the vast amount of data on the internet, you will not get distracted but waste a lot of time when gathering information. With Mind Mapping, organizing information will help you focus on what you are looking for as you will be able to collect information faster.

Strategic and Creative Thinking

In the business world, there is a huge need for strategies and creativity: this is because the two thought process helps to enhance decision-making skills. The two terms are often used together because they complement each other even though they have different meanings. While creative thinking is about finding innovative solutions to a problem, strategic thinking is about finding the right and positive methods for solving a problem.

A creative person visualizes while a strategic person analyzes; this is where Mind Mapping functions. Mind Mapping helps you to do both thinkings easily. Yes, you can do both things. You examine strategically with your left brain while you visualize creatively with your right brain. When you map different information (through analysis and visualization) around a central idea, which is the big picture, your next move or decision becomes visible. People make poor decisions by thinking with one particular side of the brain. Being creative alone is as insufficient as being strategic apart. Without Mind Maps, it is almost certain that you will make biased choices from biased thinking.

Note-Taking

Everybody takes notes from the left to the right, which is the conventional way. But is it a practical way? A lot of people will agree that traditional note-taking is boring. In most cases, people who take notes this way are often compelled to do such. Who wants to continue writing for two straight hours from left to right, up and down? It is most likely that you will miss the purpose of note-taking when you write this way. Notes are taking to store and gather new information for later use. From research, a large percentage of students who write traditionally might not use nor remember the information again.

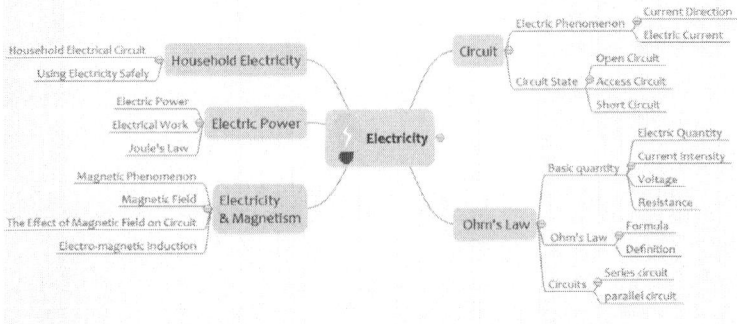

Note Taking

Taking notes with a Mind Map is very useful and exciting. It will not only help you gather information; it will make you understand the value of the information you are storing. Note-taking with Mind Maps often begins with an overview of the topic, which is in contrast to the traditional note-taking, where you can only see the big picture after the entire note. Mind Mapping notes are unconventional because you are not just writing words from left to the right; you are linking ideas or information together. Therefore, you are not bored with sentence structure as you will be using text codes, icons, and mnemonic in your note. It is difficult to add extra information on traditional notes, but with Mind Mapping notes, there are always spaces to fill in more notes. Mind Mapping note-taking is essential for gathering information faster.

Planning

Benjamin Franklin's famous planning quote keeps people on their toes. It is a simple truth: "if you fail to plan, you will plan to fail." Hence, planning has been a critical instrument for everyday living. Mind Mapping can help you plan with ease effectively. People don't fail to plan because of the time it will take and fear (uncertainties that might thwart the plan). Mind Mapping makes planning seamless. Mind Mapping is useful for planning a trip as well as planning your life: it is that simple.

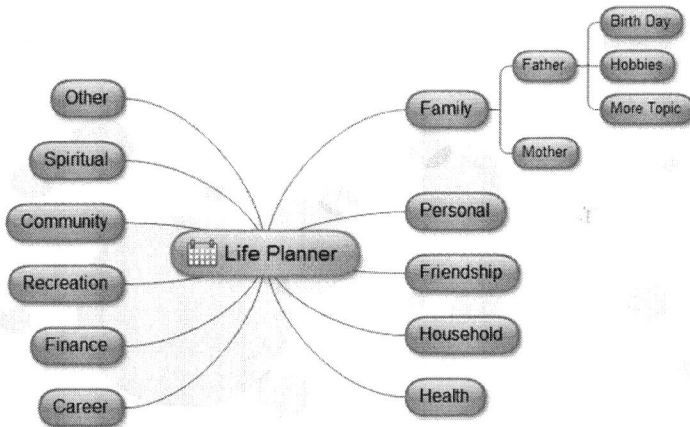

The reluctant towards planning stems from a lack of ideas. Most plans also fail for the same reason: little, no, or wrong information. The right and sufficient information are what keeps you motivated to plan and hence accomplish the goal. For instance, you want to take a vacation to Hawaii, and all you know about the city is the beautiful center of attraction it has. If this is all you know about Hawaii, there is every chance that things will not go as planned. Mind Mapping helps you get the right information that is sufficient for a plan. It makes your plan flexible, which is essential for any project that will be successful. You can't predict circumstances around your planned trip or life, but with Mind Mapping, there will be spaces that would accommodate any mishaps or troubles on the way.

Studying and Memorization

The mind needs the information to be proactive and strong. Without this strength, a man can be good as useless. Study skills are necessary for learning. After learning, it is imperative to keep your knowledge fresh in your head with memorization skills. Both skills are useful for keeping the information intact in your brain. Studying without memorizing will make you lose valuable knowledge through forgetfulness. Remembering without studying is worse will result in making stupid mistakes that will render your knowledge useless.

Since Mind Maps do not only let you write notes mindlessly, studying Mind Maps will become easy and fast. With a Mind Map note, you will easily spot the main idea as well as connect it to other purposes. If you usually read material for two hours, with Mind Mapping, you will understand the same content well for ten or twenty minutes. Also, Mind Map notes make use of icons, mnemonics, and text codes. With a note like this, memorization can never be difficult. The ideas will be easily understood and stored for use later. The only drawback here is that you will realize your Mind Map better than anyone else, which means that anyone trying to study your Mind Map notes might not benefit from it.

Presentation

Mind Mapping is all about making exciting info-graphics. When you practice mind-mapping often, you are equally becoming better at presentation. Presentation is the unique method you use in delivering information. Excellent presentation is always exceptional, well-structured, full of information, and easy to understand. Traditionally, if you are to fix all these factors in one writing or speech, it will be very long and tedious. As a result, one key factor that makes a good presentation is interest. Mind Maps presentations will not just provide structured information; it will draw people in and make them effectively understand in minutes what would have striven to realize in hours.

Most people build their presentation skills while Mind Mapping. It is challenging to learn a presentation when you have never tried Mind Mapping. Except you work on templates, making excellent presentations requires time and effort because you aim to simplify bulky information. All of these are easy when you learn Mind Mapping techniques.

Presentations are often created with PowerPoint or Prezi. You might find it challenging to use these tools; try a pencil and paper for your first Mind Map, and remember that the central idea of information is the most important thing. With this, you will finish your first presentation in minutes.

Project Management

So, you are about to manage a project, which means you have to plan, make decisions, control outcomes all to successfully complete the project within a set of time. Managing a project is a daunting task, and it is always important to find the best tools to use throughout the process. The goal of managing a project is to achieve the best results, and so, it is not just managing or surviving the process; it is about accomplishing. A good project manager must consider the time, cost, and quality of the project: all of which point to the fact that he will most likely fail if he does not use the best tool that puts every factor into consideration.

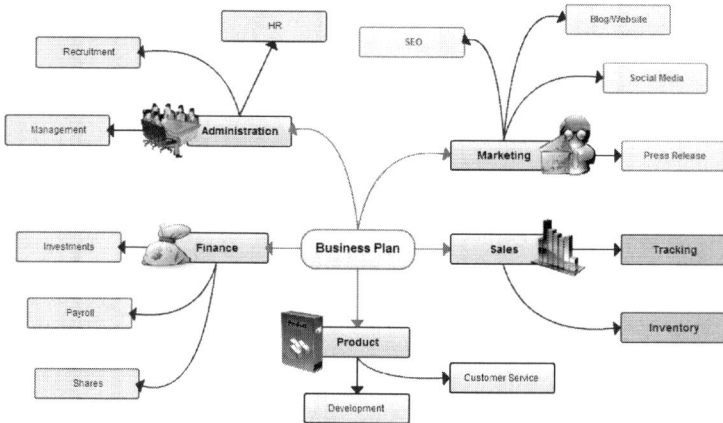

Mind Mapping is an ideal tool for project managers. Most of the applications of Mind Mapping are focuses on project managing. A project manager that can form Mind Mapping habits will be successful. The reason is that Mind Mapping reveals and expands every idea; it is an analytical yet creative approach; it makes decision making easy as it helps you continuously gather information. The bigger your project is, the bigger your Mind Maps will be. Without a doubt, every project manager needs to build Mind Maps consistently.

Evaluating Situations

Poor decisions are a result of poor judgment: prejudging or misjudging. These poor methods of judging are a result of outdated knowledge or reluctant to update our information. In simpler terms, you will make the wrong decisions if you don't evaluate correctly. Mind Maps will not only show you the central idea, and it will tell you how concepts are related. It will help you objectively weigh one idea over another. With this, you become better equipped to make the right decisions on a situation.

The first part of Mind Mapping evaluation helps you weigh the strengths and weaknesses of two or more ideas. From this evaluation, you will be to view your ideas objectively: not from the angle of preference but strength.

The second part of Mind Mapping evaluation weighs the process involved in acting on these ideas. You should also consider the procedures, tasks, and resources that would be used to execute different plans. Therefore, you will not only discover the importance of an idea, but you will also find out the ease in experimenting with each thought.

Chapter 3: Mind Mapping Techniques

Mind Mapping improves our lives in so many ways, and its effects are visible when we apply the techniques. The applications of Mind Mapping are in two categories: Learning or Studying and Memory. In summary, making an idea map can either help you to learn or study faster through note-taking, organizing information and evaluating problems. Mind Mapping can also help you remember more quickly through brainstorming, creative, and strategic thinking.

Mind Mapping techniques allow us to develop our research and memory skills effectively. Mind Mapping, unarguably one of the best methods of recording your thoughts and bringing them to exist in visual form, is undoubtedly a useful graphic tool for improving human performance, offering a universal key to unlocking the imagination and ability of your mind in a powerful way.

The technique of Mind Mapping is created to be an efficient way of producing ideas through interaction. It transforms an enormous list of dull or repetitive details into a highly structured, colorful, and exciting visual representation following the standard way of doing things in the brain. Mind Maps help to show how different pieces of information or different ideas are connected with creative problem-solving.

Therefore, Mind Mapping techniques can be divided into these two aspects:

- Mind Mapping Memory Technique (MMMT)
- Mind Mapping Study Technique (MMOST)

The two methods will help you achieve one thing: unlock brainpower. Therefore, learning the two techniques is very important so that you will not only store information in your head; you will also be able to retrieve that information whenever you need it.

The first technique is often ignored as people are interested in acquiring more knowledge. As a rule, you can only use the information you remember and not the one you just learned. Mind experts believe that people are only fascinated by new information and ideas, which means that only the old ideas that can be retrieved are essential.

The Mind Mapping Memory Technique utilizes images that can be used to retrieve information. It also uses symbols to assist people in location an idea. But, the important thing about this technique is linking. The belief that people can use repetition to remember is wrong. Recollecting an old thought is often active by relating or connecting it with another powerful view.

The second aspect of Mind Mapping technique is equally essential in gathering information. There is so much irrelevant information in the world today, which is why it is so easy to get the wrong information. The Mind Mapping Study Technique, which is also known as MMOST – Mind Mapping Organic Study Technique will help you gather valuable information and even help you store them faster. MMOST will improve your note-taking skills, study skills, organizational skills, and presentation skills.

The most important aspect of the Study Technique, which is the basis of Mind Mapping, is the addition of important links to additional topics of an idea. MMOST is created to help you add website links, books, journals, or news where you can gather related topics.

The Mind Mapping Memory Technique (MMMT)

One of the fascinating parts of the human body is the memory. Think of human memory as a large room used for storing files. The room has many cabinets, each filled files (memory). And, most importantly, they are arranged in a sophisticated manner like a neural super-computer. But, that is just half of the picture. The human memory is more complicated and sophisticated than that. The real description of the memory painted before does not consider biological and psychological insights. The truth is that human memory is a lot more complicated.

Another truth you should keep in mind is that memory is not unique; it is perfect. Experts say that, contrary to popular belief, memories are never lost or forgotten. All it requires is a key (trigger or connection) that unlocks the file (memory), which we can discover if we learn a memory technique.

How the Memory works

To start with, there are two types of memory, which is based on their storage capacity (there are different categories of human memory): short-term memory and long-term memory.

The short-term is the brain's note pad. It is used to jot down small pieces of information that may or may not be relevant for use later. The information in this memory is for the moment, and well, if you ever feel like you have forgotten something, this is where it happens.

The long-term memory is where the main events of your life enter. It takes information from the short-term memory and stores it forever. Information stored here cannot be forgotten but can only be challenging to retrieve. While information is stored in the short-term memory through sounds, images, inferences, and references, information is stored in the long-term memory through significant events and consistent retrieval of data from the short-term memory, which is where the MMMT will store information.

The Process of Remembering

The way the human memory remembers (or retrieve) information is mind-blowing. Remembrance is either done by direct retrieval or hierarchical inference. The memory is not like a scan which goes through your memory in search of information. Of course, this would mean that it would take hours of brain hibernation before anything can be recollected, which is wrong because, in most cases, we remember spontaneously.

Direct retrieval of information is possible through a question or a cue: this can be used on your Mind Map as you add inquiries to the information you gather. Hierarchical inference, which is what MMMT is all about, is done by relating information to different pieces of an idea: this explains why you quickly remember how hungry (the main idea) you are when you see your favorite meal (the smaller link).

The two processes can be achieved by:

1. Physically recognizing the link or being in contact with something related to the primary information. Recognition is the relationship of an occasion or physical item with one recently experienced or experienced and includes a procedure of examination of data with memory. For example, you recognize through perceiving a known face, genuine/false or numerous decision questions, and so on.

2. Thinking or recalling a reality, occasion, or item that isn't physically present at the moment (in the feeling of recovering a portrayal, mental picture, or idea). It requires the immediate unveiling of ideas from memory, for example, recalling the name of a perceived individual, fill-in-the gap questions, and so forth.

Consider the following memory tools:

Natural Retrievals

Dreams: these are happenings that are not real but are very vivid. Almost all humans have had dreams before. Dreams are not as practical because they are the result of our wandering unconscious mind. However, the images and videos in the dream seem real.

Hypnosis: the consciousness of hypnotized people is awake. During those hypnotic moments, their minds can wander off to events that have happened for years. Some hypnotized people often recall tales of their childhood.

Sudden and spontaneous recall: sometimes, the human memory can, for a brief moment, jolt back in time to another moment in the past. Most of these sudden experiences are caused when we go to an old place. Something about the smell or sound can make you suddenly recall old events.

Near-Death Experiences: The fear of death can awaken the mind. These brief moments that make you become suddenly aware that you about to die will bring your thoughts to the best highlights of your life. Most people with a terminal illness often use this experience to calm their minds.

These are natural examples that prove the fact that, no matter how long an event may be, we can remember it.

Other Memory Retrieving Tools

Pictures: human memory is always triggered by images. Microsoft utilized the power of pictures, and this paved the way for all forms of company icons, logos, and corporate designs.

The saying that 'a picture paints a thousand words' is true. Most company logos are self-explanatory. You can learn how to operate sophisticated machines by just following the diagrams on the logo, and this is proof of the fact that pictures are universal and cannot be affected by the language barrier. The MMMT makes use of images and colors, which makes up a picture.

Mnemonics: Mnemonics is termed the 'Mneme' technique. 'Mneme' is the god of memory is ancient Greece. These techniques were used by ancient philosophers to enhance their learning. Today, the use of mnemonics is becoming popular in schools. For instance, most of us are familiar with the use of ROYGBIV to remember the seven colors that constitute the beautiful rainbow.

Ancient Greek philosophers discovered that two main factors could improve human memory – image and association. Today, Buzan helps us to develop this idea through Mind Mapping. The British psychologist believes that the use of mnemonics can be enhanced by some factors known collectively as SMASHIN SCOPE (which is also a mnemonic). The SMASHIN stands for Sensuality, Movement, Association, Sexuality, Humor, Imagination, and Number. The SCOPE stands for Symbolism, Color, Order, Positive Images, and Exaggeration.

Using the Mind Mapping Memory Technique

Many people often wonder if this is possible: learning a memory technique. It is possible! Mind Maps are created to help your memory recall information easily. Tony Buzan, the man who popularized the idea, has written on the subject of human memory.

According to the psychologist, it starts with the five senses of perception: sound, smell, taste, sight, and touch. Using the senses can improve your memory to no small extent. It is essential always to use these senses while gathering information for your Mind Map.

Sight: use your inner eyes to create mind pictures that are related to the information you want for Mind Mapping. MMMT helps you to store images link an idea which you can continue to remember any time you see this image. Even the kind of color used in the Mind Map can help you remember an idea. For instance, if your idea revolves around a boat. You can begin to visualize the sea and its color, the boat's intensity, or even attach an event where people are sailing on the ship to the idea. When you Mind Map with these visuals, always use colors, images, charts, or graphs that will make you easily remember the idea.

Sound: you can add the perception of music to your MMMT by sound effects surrounding the idea. Making a Mind Map podcast with your phone is not a bad idea. Record the idea and the image you painted around it. Another method is to attach a video clip or an Mp3 file to your Mind Map.

Smell: enhance your memory Mind Map by including a scent you can easily relate with. For instance, based on the boat idea, you can link it to the smell of a fish.

Touch and Taste: the perception of taste and touch can also boost your memory. Include the feel or taste of anything related to the main idea.

When you incorporate the five senses into your Mind Mapping Memory Technique, the information will be retrieved with ease whenever you need it. Therefore, this is an important step to be familiar with before you start Mind Mapping. The reason is that your Mind Maps become very efficient when you store and present your information, including the five senses imagery, mnemonics, and other memory retrieving tools.

The Mind Mapping Organic Study Technique (MMOST)

Building the memory with the first technique is an essential part of gathering information. Once again, you can only use the information you remember – this is the rule. However, how can you collect information and, afterward, filter it: the important ones away from the fluffs. Well, the simple answer is to read! You can buy a textbook on the relationship and know about a relationship; you have to read the book.

Finding the motivation to read a book is challenging. Most university students who are always involved in information gathering will tell you how hard it is to keep the motivation when going through a tremendous volume resource. People decide to find quiet places, clean up their reading space and get all the necessary reading materials, but all these won't determine if you will read efficiently (if you will even read anything at all).

The Mind Mapping Organic Studying Technique was created by the man genius behind Mind Mapping itself, Tony Buzan. The technique is an ideal way to gather information faster and easier.

The process of MMOST can be divided into two steps: Preparation and Application

Preparation

The first approach is essential and must never be ignored as it seeks to build the right perspective for the information you want to gather. This involves:

- A cursory look through the material
- Knowing when you will stop your research (timing) and how much you're planning to study
- Mind Mapping the basic ideas that you are already familiar with
- Making inquiries or research questions and setting goals.

Looking Through the Material

This first action is more like when you are in a book shop flicking through the pages of a book you are thinking about purchasing. Get a brief idea of what the book entails by taking note of its structure, format, and use of charts and thickness of content. This will give you a decent review of the idea of the material that you are going to read.

Set Deadlines

The most dispiriting aspect of learning is when we are being confronted with a large volume of resources for reading and digesting. Even though we are aware that the book has an end, it is still tough to see the end of this task. The large books can be very stressful, especially when the pressure to finish it mounts. The fact is that the brain enjoys the thrills of completing tasks. Therefore, to give it this refreshing feel, it is best to allocate a reading time and a specific part of the book you want to complete. With this, the brain will be energized to complete every reading task.

Mind Map

This is an integral part of the learning process of planning and must never be neglected or ignored. Now that you've known some things after skimming through the material map, the basic idea that you know. It will not take you up to five minutes to plan the basic idea that you can remember. By writing this quick map, you are trying to bring out information from short-term memory. When you don't know an idea that you think you already know, don't waste your time trying to beat yourself around it because you might recollect later.

Make Inquiries and State What You Want From a Book

You might or might not disagree with this claim, but you do not need all the information in a particular book. Some parts of the book will require more in-depth studying than the rest, and this section of the MMOST preparation will help you determine from the course precisely what you want. The questioning aspect will help you set targets and also help with a summary of the things you need from the text.

The inquiries you make and the goals you set will bring out the critical parts of the whole text. It is like reading a book with a more definite purpose. Your mind gets attracted to the parts you have decided to learn.

The preparation step should take a little more than ten minutes to complete, after which you will ready for the next level – Application.

Application

Let's get started:

Overview

Skimming through a book will only give you a feel of the book: this is the first step in preparation. You should overview the entire text if you want to go a little beyond skimming. The overview step involves two things: visual memory and feeling memory. The visual memory helps you store the contents, diagrams, and graphs of the book. The feeling memory helps you to save any point that you easily comprehend while you make an overview. A book can be 500 pages long. If you don't make an overview, you might struggle to complete such a book, which could have had a 20-page summary that will contain the essential part of the book.

Preview

Now is the time to do a little digging into the material. To preview a book, you will make an appraisal of the language structure of the book: this involves the introduction and conclusion of paragraphs and chapters. The opening and conclusion are essential parts of each chapter in a book; they will have vital information about the book. Once again, don't be tempted to read the whole book as you can quickly get tired of it. More so, the questions you ask will help you locate vital information faster.

In-view

By this time, the entire book would have been reduced to small bits. Read the remaining parts, which is similar to filling the gaps of a puzzle. Do not forget that you don't need all the information in a book. So, it is advisable to take what is required and ignore the rest.

Review

If you have previously stated the goal you want to achieve from studying a book, this is the time to know if you have found what you are looking for. Has the book answered all your inquiries? Can it solve the problem you hope to resolve?

Mind Map – Note-taking

Since Mind Mapping itself should already be seen as a habit, this should not be new to you. The Mind Map you create at this stage helps you to present the entire book effectively in a simple model. No matter how bulky the book is, you can create a simple Mind Map that explains the book in simpler terms.

Continuous Reading is the Key

Most people have reiterated that MMOST is not a useful technique for studying: this is the problem of many people who read a book and do not profit from it. What step did they miss in studying? Learning is a continuous process. There is saying that goes thus: 'A man that stops learning, starts dying.' When gathering information, you must understand that the purpose is to use the information. And to use information, you must be familiar with it. As you now know, you must continue reading and reviewing a book until your mind is wrapped around it firmly.

MMOST is very effective for studying: this; you will use for note-taking, information gathering, and presentation applications in Mind Mapping. The process might feel a little off when you start, but as you practice these techniques together, applying Mind Mapping will become easy.

In conclusion, the advantages of implementing the Mind Mapping technique in your everyday routine are enormous. Everyone could become a Mind Map user or, for that matter, a Mind Map master. All you need is an appropriate Mind Mapping software to get started. iMindQ is an example of a software that offers a wide range of features for its users to get the most of this creative technique.

Starting from brainstorming and note-taking to project or event planning, studying, and public speaking or presenting, the Mind Maps can help you stimulate both the creative and logical way of thinking and encourage you to let your ideas and thoughts flow freely.

Finally, if you are using it the right way, Mind Mapping will surely stimulate your creative thinking and allow you to solve problems more effectively. You just need to follow all the previous steps we included in this guide, and you will be closer to becoming the master of Mind Mapping.

Chapter 4: 7 Easy Steps to Create an Effective Mind Map

In the previous chapters, we dived into the theoretical part of Mind Maps, where I explained what a Mind Map is, why it should be used, its applications and techniques. Now, it's time to be more practical by discussing the creation of an effective Mind Map.

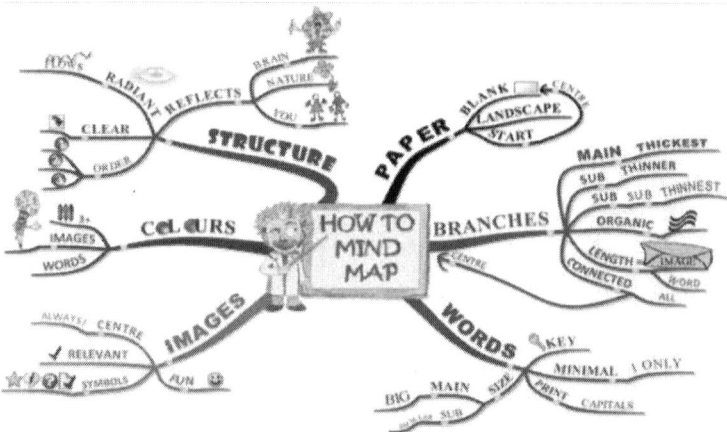

Using Mind Maps has numerous benefits in our everyday life. It is a tool that helps to simplify the process of organizing, generating, and presentation of thoughts, ideas, and information. To simplify the process of creating an effective Mind Map, we will be using a seven-step system to create and master Mind Mapping techniques.

7 Easy Steps to Master Mind Mapping Techniques

Using flashcards to memorize short ideas in a flash is effective to remember information, but if you are dealing with a more complex subject, you will be needing a study method that will help you understand, summarize and memorize all your information without spending too much time. Well, Mind Mapping is an effective study tool that can help you do all that.

I have earlier explained the importance of Mind Maps, its various uses, Mind Mapping techniques, and how to make an effective Mind Map. Now, we would be looking at seven easy steps to use to master Mind Mapping techniques effectively. Take your time to study these steps as you master your Mind Map.

Step 1: Choose Your Central Topic

The first step is the most important step to take when creating an effective Mind Map. You need to choose a central topic that is relevant. A Mind Map is used to elaborate and explore the main topic that is placed in the center of the map, which will later be mapped out into a number of topics and sub-topics. Just think of a Mind Map as a tree with many branches and sub-branches. So, your central idea needs to be the core of that tree that holds all the branches and sub-branches together.

Now, how do you choose a central topic? This depends on your purpose of creating the Mind Map. First, you need to know if your central topic will be a sentence, one specific keyword, a problem that needs solving, or a question that needs an answer. Find out, then place it at the center, in a circle, or you can decide to use a different shape that seems appropriate. Then personalize it with font, color, image, or symbol.

Step 2: Branch Out Your Map

Your topics, or let's say "branches" are the essential part of Mind Maps. These branches are used in defining the essential areas of a particular topic. To view it from another angle, a Mind Map, which has a key subject of "Travel Plan" in the center, can grow into branches and cover the basics about planning a trip; these can be budget, accommodation, transport itinerary, and agenda. Although the list of branches is determined based on your needs, and this is why a Mind Map is transformative, flexible, and versatile.

When using Mind Maps, what might work for you may not work for me or others. But as long as the Mind Map is formed with the necessary elements and following the main structure, then you can add as many branches as you like and need. The topic that is usually described with a keyword or two related to the main topic is what stimulates and inspires the creative side of the brain to create more new ideas and therefore plunge into the subject.

Step 3: Spread Out The Branches With Sub-Branches

After expanding your central topic into different topics, it's now time to split the topics further into sub-topics or let's say sub-branches. This may sound a little bit confusing, but it is quite simple. You have created a central idea that has spread into different topics; this should further grow into sub-topics. Each branch is connected to its sub-branches, and together, all of them will expand the main idea that is in the center.

If the branches are explained with a keyword or two, a diverse number of words can be in the sub-branches; although, it depends on what they are explaining. What they explain can vary from just a word to more complex sentences, if you stick to the specific keywords that are related to the main idea. Have it at the back of your mind that your Mind Map can be expanded, and where you are doesn't have to be the end. You can remove some of the existing branches or add; it all depends on your preferences.

Step 4: Expand and Grow the Sub-Branches

In terms of content, the sub-branches constitute the Mind Map, and it is what makes it complete. In fact, if you don't expand your topic and make it general, your Mind Map won't be as powerful as it should. You need to focus on elaborating on the Mind Map and the topics until you don't have anything left to add to a particular branch.

Use ideas and associations of the information you have and all of your ideas that relate to the main subject to radiate out the map. If you are done adding branches and sub-branches, you can now move to the more creative steps, which is decorating the maps with images and colors. This should make the Mind Map bold and attention-grabbing.

Step 5: Choose A Font And Start Coloring The Mind Map

A Mind Map can be an effective and powerful tool when you give the contents a more suitable font and enhance the topics and sub-topics with different shades of colors. You can use different colors to make your Mind Map personal and unique. You can customize each branch and sub-branch according to how you want it.

The role the different colors are playing here isn't just to make your Mind Map look attractive. Studies have suggested that colors have a positive impact on how humans memorize; it sharpens our memorization skills. According to studies, a person has a greater ability to memorize and remember a color than a word. So, using different colors to create a Mind Map is always better as it will make memorization of the information easier when you connect each information with color.

If you find it difficult to decide or settle for a particular color and font, you can reflect on the message you are trying to pass across or any certain parts of the content that needs to be memorized. Once you are done with this, you can now choose the colors that you find as the most powerful to highlight the content. If you want to make your Mind Map more memorable, you can underline or bold the text.

Step 6: Add Visuals To The Topics And Subtopics

By now, your Mind Map should be expanded, and the important topics and sub-topics should be emphasized in different beautiful colors. We can now move to the next step; this is usually an interesting one where you add symbols and images to the content. Earlier, I made mention of the importance of colors and how it helps with memorization, but with visuals getting involved, it provides an even better benefit to the brain. Symbols and images are usually associated with a particular idea or concept, and this can help you memorize and remember information better.

So, if your aim of using your Mind Map is to help you remember a piece of particular information, it isn't advisable to skip this step. This is an important step, especially if you are preparing a presentation with the tool or studying for an exam. Add symbols and images besides the content, and you will be surprised at how well you remember the place you placed them, and all the information that is associated with them.

Step 7: Add A Background Image To The Mind Map

Once you have created all the steps, which entails creating your Mind Map with branches and sub-branches, using colors, symbols, and images to decorate them, it will bring you to the last step of adding a background pattern or an image to your Mind Map. This will highlight the content and give your mind a statement piece look.

When you want to choose a background or an image for your Mind Map, always go for a style that matches with the main topic or idea of your Mind Map. Note, when you draw or place a background image, it makes your Mind Map more appealing and engaging to the eye. This is why this step is important and shouldn't be neglected.

In conclusion, what's the essence of creating a Mind Map if it is not shared or presented? Whether the Mind Map is for yourself or you are presenting it to your colleagues or boss, always make it as attractive as possible. Do you know that the more effort you place in the creation of the Mind Map, the more you get to benefit from it?

Mind Mapping technique is an engaging, creative, and better alternative for PowerPoint presentations. The reason is that it allows you to visually present your idea and information in a totally different format that sparks people's interest.

Note, a tree-like presentation is more likely to trigger people's minds for idea generation and creative outside the box thinking. So, always present your Mind Map in an easy and unique way.

How Mind Mapping Can Help You

Do you know that before now, Mind Maps allow you to see the **BIG** picture while engaging your whole brain? A Mind Map is an all-brain method of generating and organizing ideas that are primarily inspired by the note-taking approach of Leonardo da Vinci. However, as we pointed out earlier, the theory was pioneered by Tony Buzan.

Mind Mapping helps you to establish a logical sequence and overall content structure while encouraging creativity and spontaneity. The note-taking methods of many of the geniuses of literature include a branching, original design complemented by many drawings, imaginative doodles, and keywords. Such of these geniuses include personalities such as the Great Charles Darwin, Artistic Michelangelo, Mark Twain, and Leonardo da Vinci.

To appreciate the benefits of Mind Mapping, you probably have to understand what is it you stand to benefit. It shouldn't be overwhelming even for a novice to know more about the Mind Mapping process. The truth is that Mind Mapping is such an easy tool for learning that you don't also have to put so much stress on it!

In many different fields, Mind Maps are popular methods for training and project management. Many people have asked whether Mind Maps are as high as they are indoctrinated to students of the subject. As the old saying goes, "there are two sides to each coin." here is how Mind Maps can help you:

It Makes Planning Your Finances Easy

It's a good idea to create a Mind Map for your investments as it reveals the big picture of your overall financial life. The financial Mind Map's divisions may include items like income, expenses, debt, expenditure, retirement plan, estate plan, and so on. Then each section can be divided into sub-branches. For example, the division of "Estate Plan" could be split into Will, Revocable Living Trust, Attorney Power, Health Care Proxy, and so on. By including divisions of the third and fourth level, you can choose to add further info.

It Allows You Create To-Do Lists Effortlessly

To do this type in the middle of the page, something simple like "to do." Next, define the main categories and position them as divisions. Some examples can be a blog, work, home, and errands. Outline the activities you need to do as sub-branches for each of the classes. You may incorporate the following sub-branches for the "Post" group as an illustration: publish a blog post, spread the blog post on social media, invest 15 minutes on Twitter, visit three blogs in my niche and leave comments, and contact potential sponsors. You could further break down each assignment for a third level: add time limits for each project, include more details on the task, and so on.

Mind Maps Can Be Used to Plan Your Year

Planning can be made easy with Mind Maps. For example, write down at the center of your page the year that you intend planning for. When creating branches, know that each branch is a year goal. Let's say one of your goals for the year is to make an additional $12,000 that you'll put down to your retirement. You must split the target into four milestones; a sub-branch will represent each milestone. Here are the four sub-branches:

- By March 31, raise $3,000.
- Earn $8,000 by June 30.
- Earn $11,000 by 30 September.
- Earn $14,000 until 31 December.

And break down each achievement still. The "Earn $5,000 by March 31" sub-branch can be split down as follows:

- Earn $3,000 by January 31.
- Earn $4,000 as of February 28.
- Earn $5,000 by March 31.

These are your divisions at the third level branches. The concrete measures you're going to take to make that money can be the 4th tier divisions.

Mind Maps Can Help You Generate Ideas
Place a picture in the middle of the page that represents the subject you want to create ideas for, begin to radiate any concept that comes into your mind on this subject from that picture. For each design, build a branch. Check at the divisions and see the keyword or

image on each chapter sparking ideas. Place the new ideas as sub-branches. For each sub-branch, formulate at least three ideas and put them down as divisions of the third level. You can either start there or add a fourth stage. Look through your final Mind Map when you're done and decide which idea you'll be implementing. Subsequently, get out into the world and put forth your plan into practice.

Mind Maps Can Be Used as A Problem-Solving Technique

Insert an image in the center of a piece of paper, along with the appropriate keyword, when attempting to solve a problem. Then draw six branches out of the image/keyword center and write to each department one of the following questions:

- The Why?
- The When?
- The Where?
- The What?
- The How?
- The Who?

Address these questions making use of your Mind Map sub-branches and continue from there to openly connect approaches to the situation.

Mind Maps Help You Retain Information Gotten from Books

Many people complain that they always forget quickly what they have read in a book or learned. But there's a way to remember and keep the information in the books you're reading retained in your mind. Each time you read something, you find informative or helpful, you can retain up to 70 % of this by creating a Mind Map. The Mind Map branches can be the chapter headings of the most important chapters of the book that you have read. And after that, write down as sub-headings the main ideas of each paragraph. Branches at the third level can include illustrations, quotations, and even your thoughts about what you're learning. You can compose suggestions on the actions that the book or essay encouraged you to take in the fourth stage.

Mind Maps Can Help You in Writing E-books

If you've been trying to write an eBook for a while, but at the planning stage, you keep getting lost, a Mind Map might be just what you require. What's the subject of your eBook? Write down that at the bottom of the page and add ten different branches. Tag them as Chapter 1, Chapter 2, Chapter 3, and so on. You can incorporate every chapter's specific titles later, but write down possible topics for now. Use sub-branches of suggestions about what you will include in each section for each paragraph. Finally, write down illustrations for each of the ideas as a third level.

Mind Maps can Help You Set Life Goals

Write in the middle of the page your "Life Goals" (you can also take a picture of yourself or add a text). Select what you see as the core areas of life. These may involve leisure, fun, family, donations, employment, money, etc. Any of these will be one of the Mind Map's divisions. You can also split any aspect of your life in a way that makes sense to you. The Family branch, for instance, could be divided into the following sub-branches: parents, brothers and sisters, husband or wife, children, entire family, etc. So write down for each of the sub-branches at least three life goals. These are supposed to be the divisions of the third level. You can write down suggestions on how to accomplish each objective as fourth level branches, a timetable, the tools you're going to need, and so on.

Mind Maps Can Help You Jot Down Notes During Meetings

Anytime that you find yourself in an office meeting, kindly do the following;

- The purpose of the meeting should be written at the center of the page.
- Understand that each item on the agenda will be represented as one of the main branches that are described in your Mind Map (you should probably get a hold of the schedule before the meeting).
- During the course of the meeting, add sub-branches to each agenda item with the main points that are being discussed for

each item (such as facts, budget, facts, who will do what, and so on).

- Represent interlink items with pictures.

Mind Maps Can Help You For Your Project Management

What is the project name you will be working on? Write it down in the center of the page. What are the main tasks for the project to complete? Write them down as sub-branches. Divide the main tasks into sub-tasks and write them down as branches of the third level. You may build a fourth level for each sub-task by adding information such as length, price, necessary materials, etc.

Chapter 5: Mastering Mind Mapping

To utilize your Mind Maps and get the best out of it, there are laws and principles guiding Mind Maps that you need to put into consideration. Once you know the do's and don'ts of Mind Mapping, you should be able to master how to create it and use it effectively. First, let's take a look at some of the principles guiding Mind Maps.

Principles of Mind Mapping

Just like I have overemphasized in the earlier chapters in this guide, you will be getting a maximum benefit when you use Mind Maps in your daily life. We've gone through Mind Mapping techniques, and their applications next is the principle guiding Mind Mapping.

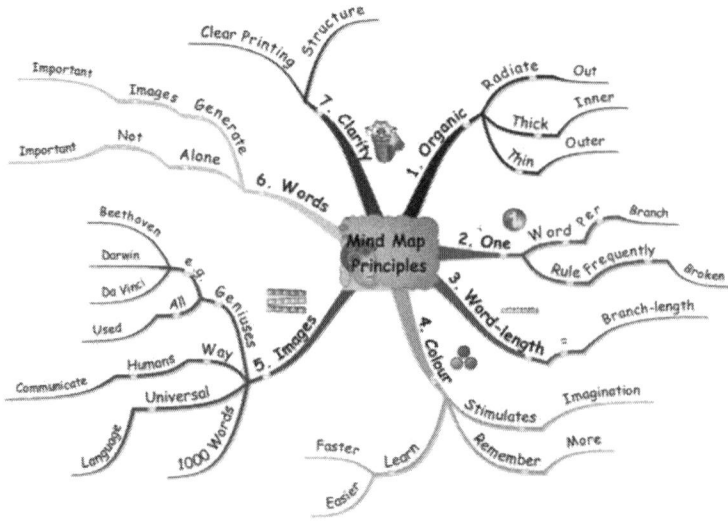

These principles of Mind Mapping should be used to guide you as you master the 7 steps.

Organic

A Mind Map should be organic in its real form, and when making use of it as a tool, use the free-flowing branches that are curved. The inner branches of the maps should be thicker as it gets closer to the center, and thinner when it radiates outwardly. In other words, the inner branches should be thicker than the outer branches.

One Word Per Line

According to the principle of the one word per line, it states that each branch should only have one word. Tony was very strict with this principle because he believed that one word per line would bring about more creativity as it makes the Mind Map "open" – as each keyword produces an infinite number of ideas and associations.

According to our experience, this principle has been broken most of the time, and this can be your greatest challenge when learning how to use Mind Maps. As users, we already have our set of rules that governs this principle, and most of the Mind Map software out there that makes it impossible to abide by this principle; in fact, it encourages you to break it.

Well, I wouldn't want us to be dogmatic, so it's up to you to decide for yourself once you have finished this guide and gained some experience with using Mind Maps.

Word Length

Your word length should be equal to the branch length. The reason behind this is because it ensures the link between the word length and branch length is maintained; this makes it easier to be remembered.

Color

When we see something colorful, it stimulated our imagination, and this makes it easier for us to remember things. We get to learn faster and easier, too, if colors are used. In fact, it makes the Mind Mapping process more fun!

Images

Remember the saying that says, "A picture is worth more than a thousand words?" Well, we can refer to pictures as a universal language and how humans communicate. All the notable geniuses the world has had have used images in their note. From Da Vinci, Beethoven, and even Darwin.

Words are Not Important

Don't get me wrong here when I say the word is not important. Just that, when it is just words, it is not important. The most important is the images the words have created. So, choose words that give a clearer image of what you want to remember.

Clarity

When you structure and print your mind clearly, you will be having clarity of thinking and well-structured thoughts. So, clarity is important.

Finally, just like with most disciplines in life, sticking to the principles of the concept (Mind Map) when you create it will definitely give you the best results. If you ever need to break the principles guiding Mind Maps, then wait till you have experience with using it. The experience will teach you how to obey rules and when you can break them.

How to Mind Map Using Tony Buzan's 10 Laws of Mind Mapping

Tony Buzan, who is generally referred to as the father of the Mind Map, gave 10 laws to follow to create a good Buzan type or classical Mind Map. Follow these laws and make sure you don't break them.

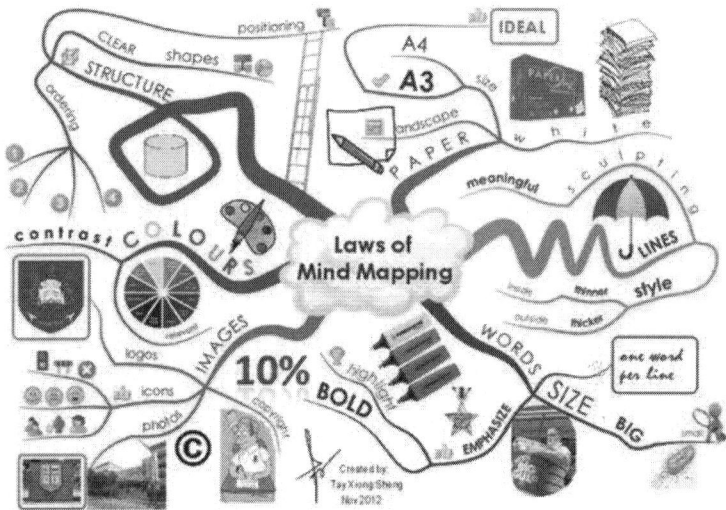

First Law: Blank Paper in The Landscape Orientation

This law of Tony Buzan states that a blank paper should be in the landscape orientation, but why is using a blank paper so important? Let's say it is because the chemical composition of our brain is more related to paper than the computer. The inner landscape of our brain isn't lined, and when you make use of a lined paper, you are forming a barrier between your thoughts and the law.

Landscape orientation is also important because we tend to see more horizontally than vertically. A peripheral vision is more accessible when it's left to right than up and down. The landscape orientation also allows a better mirroring of a clock – this is an essential structure. But what is this clock, you may ask? It is the clock's formation that allows us to immediately turn a Mind Map to a memory palace just at a glance.

Second Law: Draw A Central Image in The Center

According to Tony Buzan, the central image of our Mind Maps should have at least three colors. This is a very subtle point that most of us have missed many times. Well, to master your Mind Maps better, put it into practice, the more and observe your improvements. The image used should be able to express your core concern.

Third Law: Different Images Should Appear Throughout the Mind Map

When drawing your Mind Maps, use dimensions. For example, you can draw some of your keywords in 3D.

Fourth Law: Keywords Should Be Capitalized

For reasons still unknown to me, this law can be a very difficult one to follow. Was it because we were already ditching the rules during our high school days or read too many cummings those days. Well, for more emphasis, keywords should be capitalized.

Fifth Law: Each Keyword Should Have Its Own "Branch"

This law will help you go far in the mastering of mind if adhered to. Though it can be counterintuitive if you are a wordy sound-conceptual person, it works as it forms pressure on the keyword and even on your mind.

Just think of it like this: if you are looking at a clump of sentences and you start reading, you are indirectly assisting your memory in a way that it turns it off. You don't need to remember what your Mind Map has encoded if you can remember what you say. If you have a keyword, you are giving your brain a memory workout creatively. This brain exercise will result in success.

Sixth Law: Your Branches Should Flow and Taper

When you look closely at an image of the neural network of your brain, you will see precisely the tapering that Tony Buzan wants us to benefit from when using Mind Maps. This sixth law shows that Mind Mapping mirrors our brain. The more we bring our mind and Mind Map together in flow and structure, the more our memory and creativity perform.

Seventh Law: Balance The Length of Your Branches

Balancing the length of your branches is a law that needs more attention. However, by following the other laws, adhering to this law will naturally take its course.

Eighth Law: Use Tons of Colors

A lot of people have struggled to keep to this law; I also had issues with this. Sometimes, choosing the right colors to use can stir up a bit of anxiety in you, especially when you start asking yourself questions like, which color to use, what if you made a mistake, or if a particular color is appropriate for the idea.

There is a reason our brain pumps out these questions, but if you use tons of color, you will see that you will be making the right decisions.

Ninth Law: Emphasize Points with Arrows and Lines

Connecting different branches with arrows is one fun part for me. It shows the points clearly.

Tenth Law: Maximize The Clarity of Blank Space/White Space

For me, this is the last and most captivating law of Mind Mapping. It involves using blank space for clarity – let your Mind Maps "breath."

Finally, some laws are made to be broken, but in this case, there is an exception. Make sure you don't break these laws as they are the needed tools that will help you quickly master your Mind Map without making mistakes.

The Whole-Brain Thinking

I believe that by now, you should have a good understanding of mind maps and how useful they can be. They are a multi-purpose tool, flexible enough that you can use them for anything you want to. Also, mind maps help you think smarter by opening up your mind and grants you access to more brainpower.

There is a theory about how humans can think optimally. It is known as the 'Whole Brain Thinking.' Mind maps can stimulate your mind and allow whole-brain thinking to occur, enabling you to think smarter, faster, and better.

The Whole-Brain Thinking states that humans think in four particular ways which are:

- Logical Thinking: This way of thinking focuses on facts and bottom lines
- Creative Thinking: This particular way of thinking sees the big picture of things and likes to be fun or have fun
- Practical Thinking: This way of thinking leans towards the organization of things, and follow through or take action
- Rational Thinking: This way of thinking, usually tunes into the thinking of the person and that of others

The 'Whole Brain Thinking' theory suggests that some people are more logical, while others are more creative, some are more practical, and some tend to be more reliant on their feelings.

However, we all have the ability to be a logical, creative, practical, or rational – we can think in each of the ways mentioned before. Even though we do think in one way or the other, in truth, all the four ways of thinking are all connected and work in sync with each other.

Logical thinking focuses on facts and the bottom line. It is a way of thinking that enables us to rationalize things like if x = y and y = z, and 'x' must equal 'z' as well. Creative thinking, on the other hand, helps us to see the bigger picture of things. It is also that part of us that enables us to play, be lively, and have fun.

Our rational thinking mind enables us to tune into our own emotions and feelings as well as that of others, and this is also related to how we handle both tangible and intangible things around us. Therefore, we can relate to several ideas and concepts in the same way we do relate to other people. Also, practical thinking enables us to organize and take the necessary actions properly.

Mind maps are special, and one of the reasons why they are so important is because they connect with all of these forms of thinking or thoughts. Mind mapping enables us to clearly see how several concepts, ideas, and different forms of thoughts that fit with each other in a logical manner. Mind maps help you see the entire picture at a glance because it taps into the creative aspect of our thinking. Besides, mind mapping enables us to formulate great ideas and play around with various concepts. So, it grabs the creative aspect of our mind, as well.

Our rational thoughts help us to see the relationships that exist among various items and concepts, which is an essential process of mind mapping. Understanding these relationships helps us to effectively organize our thoughts and also develop our ideas in a logical way. When we think rationally, we are indeed mapping things out. Most of the things we write out usually correlates to how we feel things in general as our creative mind is busy generating ideas. Practical reasoning pushes us to organize the information on a mind map, make it into a useable tool, and take the necessary action.

So far, you would have realized that all the forms of thinking work in concert with each other, and to a certain degree, are interconnected with each other. Mind mapping enables us to open, expand, and explore each of these forms of thinking and allow them to flow and work in better harmony with one another.

All the four thinking forms are tapped into when you review information on a mind map, which is also why it is quite easy to learn from mind maps. It engages the entire brain – it enables whole-brain thinking.

Mind maps are designed to be able to represent any form of information. They are created to be used in diverse ways, handle and accomplish any type of task through them. Mind maps can hold a plethora of information, including images, charts, arrows, and many more. Mind maps turn a complex system of information into something that can be easily understood. Hence, it tasks your mind to think on a much higher level than you would normally do.

If you are still to use a mind map, you really should give it a try now. You can simply begin with a sheet paper, and start your journey of mind mapping and experience this amazing tool for yourself. That way, you could have the first-hand experience about the amazing things mind maps could do for you and the so many ways you can apply them.

Mind maps contain an unlimited amount of planning, gathering, organizing, and deciphering of information that can be helpful in improving your business, career, relationships, ideas, and life as a whole.

Conclusion

We have come to the end of this guide; thank you for making it through to the end of *How to Mind Map,* let's hope that the information has been able to provide you with all the tools you need to create an effective and powerful Mind Map.

The next step to take is to jot down some important points you have learned, and put the laws guiding creating an effective Mind Map into practice, and always make reference to this guide when you are not clear about something.

Some Mind Mapping software has helped people to simplify the process of creating a Mind Map, but know that you are the best software to improve your memory and creativity skills. After all, our brain system and that of the computer both involve information to be chemically encoded. And for computers to bring out lots of possible outcomes, it needs to follow the rules, and the same with the creation of Mind Maps I have explained in this guide.

Mind Maps are an efficient technique for organizing thought processes around complex areas, be it in business or daily life. There have been several case studies on Mind Mappings taking part in workshops, learning a new subject, and recognizing an existing program; this shows that Mind Maps can be beneficial to you in different ways. With the information provided in this guide and putting in lots of practice, your Mind Mapping will become more effective and powerful.

More by Troye Bates

Discover all books from the Brain Training Series by Troye Bates at:

bit.ly/troye-bates

Book 1: *How to Improve Memory*

Book 2: *How to Read Faster*

Book 3: *How to Focus Your Mind*

Book 4: *How to Learn Faster*

Book 5: *How to Study Effectively*

Book 6: *How to Mind Map*

Book 7: *How to Think Differently*

Book 8: *How to Rewire Your Brain*

Themed book bundles available at discounted prices:

bit.ly/troye-bates

Printed in Great Britain
by Amazon